THE ATKINS DIET

Set Yourself Up for Success

INTRODUCTION

I want to thank you and congratulate you for downloading the book, *"The Atkins Diet, Set Yourself Up for Success"*.

This book contains proven steps and strategies on how to get properly started on the Atkins diet and how to maintain it for as long as you like.

The Atkins diet has been around since 1972, but it's had a few great changes in the recent past. You'll learn how the new Atkins diet differs from the original and from the version folks were practicing in the 1990s, as well as how you can adapt the current healthier interpretation to your personal lifestyle. The Atkins diet is a proven way to lose weight quickly and to keep it off long term. Some people find they like the health benefits of this diet so much they stay on it for the rest of their lives!

Thanks again for downloading this book, I hope you enjoy it!

©Copyright 2016 by SAM PUBLISHING
All rights reserved.

This document is geared towards providing exact and reliable information in regards to the topic and issue covered. The publication is sold with the idea that the publisher is not required to render accounting, officially permitted, or otherwise, qualified services. If advice is necessary, legal or professional, a practiced individual in the profession should be ordered.

From a Declaration of Principles which was accepted and approved equally by a Committee of the American Bar Association and a Committee of Publishers and Associations.

In no way is it legal to reproduce, duplicate, or transmit any part of this document in either electronic means or in printed format. Recording of this publication is strictly prohibited and any storage of this document is not allowed unless with written permission from the publisher. All rights reserved.

The information provided herein is stated to be truthful and consistent, in that any liability, in terms of inattention or otherwise, by any usage or abuse of any policies, processes, or directions contained within is the solitary and utter responsibility of the recipient reader. Under no circumstances will any legal responsibility or blame be held against the publisher for any reparation, damages, or monetary loss due to the information herein, either directly or indirectly.

Respective authors own all copyrights not held by the publisher.

The information herein is offered for informational purposes solely, and is universal as so. The presentation of the information is without contract or any type of guarantee assurance.

The trademarks that are used are without any consent, and the publication of the trademark is without permission or backing by the trademark owner. All trademarks and brands within this book are for clarifying purposes only and are the owned by the owners themselves, not affiliated with this document.

Contents

Introduction...2

Introduction...2

Chapter : The Atkins Diet Basics..6

Chapter 2 : How the Atkins Diet Compares to Other 8

Chapter 3 : What's New with the Atkins Diet? 10

Chapter 4 : Benefits of the Atkins Diet 14

Chapter 5 : Misconceptions About the Atkins Diet................18

Chapter 6 : The Structure of the Atkins Diet.....................21

Chapter 7 :Starting the Atkins Diet................................25

Chapter 8 : Foods to Which You Will Bid Farewell................28

Chapter 9 : Shopping for the Atkins Diet.........................30

Chapter 10 : A Typical Daily Menu on Atkins 34

Chapter 11 : Beverages on Atkins 37

Chapter 12 : Sample Recipes for the Atkins Diet.................40

Chapter 13 : Eating Your Favorite Foods on the Atkins 43

Chapter 14 : Tips for Staying on the Atkins Diet 46

Chapter 15 : Dealing with Weight Loss Plateaus..................50

Conclusion 54

CHAPTER 1

The Atkins Diet Basics

The Atkins diet was developed in the 1960s by Robert Atkins as a solution to his own weight problem. His diet plan was based largely on a study published in the *Journal of the American Medical Association* in which patients lost more weight on a low-carbohydrate diet than with other food plans. Atkins published his first book on the topic in 1972 and another in 2002 promoting the same regimen. The Atkins diet was updated and revised in 2010 (see "What's New with the Atkins Diet," below), but it has remained essentially a low-carbohydrate, high-fat, moderate- to high-protein diet.

The theory behind the Atkins diet is that by only consuming a limited amount of carbohydrates (sugars and starches), dieters' glucose (blood sugar) levels stay more even, and the body burns fat as a fuel source, making this a good weight loss mechanism.

There are added benefits to this diet for many people, including better regulation of insulin (the hormone that helps metabolize glucose) and a reduction in food cravings that result from precipitous drops in blood sugar. If you've ever experienced that sudden lightheaded, nauseous feeling of needing to eat something starchy right away, the Atkins diet may be well worth your consideration. Likewise, if you have extra pounds you'd like to drop, the Atkins diet may be a good plan for you.

As you'll learn in Chapter 6, the Atkins diet uses a very systematic regimen for deciding what you can and cannot eat. There are several pathways you can follow with the diet, but each one starts out with a fairly restricted list of allowed foods and gradually adds back foods over time. There are some foods, however, that are never allowed on the Atkins diet, and these are outlined for you in Chapter 8.

How you add back food on the Atkins diet is determined by several things:

- how you feel at any given stage of the diet

- your weight loss progress

- the desire to maintain your current weight

- food sensitivities that you discover while withholding certain foods

You may feel like you're not getting adequate nutrients or have enough energy, in which case it may make sense to add certain elements back to your diet. Or you may have reached your weight loss goals and need to switch to a caloric intake to stay at your current weight. Perhaps you'll start training for a 5K or a marathon, so your nutritional needs will change accordingly.

Adding back foods methodically allows you to see if specific foods cause your weight loss to plateau or cause you symptoms of discomfort. You may find that you feel better with some foods eliminated from your diet permanently, such as if you have intolerance for gluten, found in things like pasta and bread. The beauty of the Atkins diet is that it is superbly well organized, so you can fine tune it to your unique needs and tastes and stay on the diet for a lifetime if you so desire.

CHAPTER 2

How the Atkins Diet Compares to Other Low-Carb Regimens

There are a number of low-carb diets being advocated today, and it can be confusing to keep them all straight. You may be wondering how the Atkins Diet compares to similar plans you've heard about like:

- the Paleo diet

- the ketogenic diet

- general low-carb regimens

If you drew a diagram of all of these diets, there would certainly be areas where they overlap with each other. Diets that are simply called "low-carb" also limit the intake of carbohydrates, but they are less controlled about it than the Atkins diet. Carbohydrate percentages can vary widely, as can the ratios of protein and fat consumed.

The Paleo diet is like the Atkins diet in that it also limits carbohydrates. This is because the Paleo diet is modeled after what Paleolithic humans purportedly ate before the development of agriculture. Foods that were obtained by hunting and gathering, like meat, nuts, and berries, are cornerstones of the Paleo diet, while grain products and dairy are generally forbidden (some Paleo dieters do eat butter).

The exclusion of dairy products makes the Paleo diet different from Atkins. Like general low-carb diets, the Paleo diet is usually also somewhat less systematic in its approach to ratios of fat, protein, and carbohydrates. Some Paleo dieters may by default wind up following a version of the

Atkins diet, but they may also pursue a vastly different food plan.

The ketogenic diet is yet another low-carb diet, but it promotes very high fat consumption and moderate protein intake. It was developed nearly 100 years ago as a way to control epileptic seizures in children, and while it is still used for that purpose, it is also used as a weight loss plan.

The ketogenic diet permanently limits carbohydrates in such a way that the body switches from burning glucose to using fat as its primary fuel source. This is referred to as being "in ketosis," which is different than being in ketoacidosis, a dangerous state that can arise in diabetes.

Many followers of the Atkins diet actually find themselves in ketosis during the induction phase of the diet (see Chapter 6). This is why they see dramatic weight loss almost immediately and also why they may not feel so well during the first week or so of the diet, as the body adjusts to this metabolic shift. Atkins dieters who stay in the induction phase for a prolonged period—if they have a great deal of weight to lose, for example—stay in ketosis during that time as well. When more carbohydrates are added back into the diet, however, being in ketosis is usually no longer possible.

Some dieters find it's easier to maintain the Atkins diet long term than a ketogenic diet, which is more restrictive. The changes made to the Atkins diet over the last decade have made it more user friendly. While both the ketogenic and Atkins diets require some willpower to get through their respective initial stages, being able to add many foods back to the diet later makes the Atkins diet a bit easier to maintain over time.

CHAPTER 3

What's New with the Atkins Diet?

The Atkins diet received a fair bit of skepticism and criticism when it first debuted in the early '70s and was touted again in the '90s. Most of the doubt centered around the diet's mandate of high fat consumption at the expense of carbohydrates. At that time, butter was considered bad and whole grain breads were thought to be good for you, regardless of the circumstances.

Now, however, recent medical studies have shown that high-fat, low-carbohydrate diets are actually healthier for most individuals, provided they eat enough protein and get all the micronutrients they need, like vitamins and minerals.

It's not that butter, whole grains, or other foods are all good or all bad in and of themselves. It's how they are consumed together and in what quantities that determines how most people's bodies react to them. The common Western diet has become very high in carbohydrates that many people don't need because they are more sedentary than in the past. Also, portion size has increased. Excess carbohydrates are easily converted to and stored as fat in the human body, which is unhealthy and aesthetically displeasing to most people.

A high-carbohydrate, high-fat diet is an even worse combination, which had unfortunately become the norm for many people towards the end of the 20th Century. These carbohydrates weren't usually in the form of fruits, vegetables, and unrefined grains either; they were highly processed foods, with many of their redeeming qualities stripped from them before they ever reached the dining room table.

Consuming processed carbohydrates together with a lot of

dietary fat is the easiest way to guarantee they will both be stored on the body as fat cells. Too many carbohydrates stimulate excess insulin production, and instead of metabolizing the carbs, the body turns them into fat. If you're not burning the fat you eat, it gets stored on the body right along with all those extra carbs.

Enter the low-fat diet craze in the 1980s and '90s. The medical establishment and many food manufacturers thought fat was the big problem, and it should be removed from the equation. Low-fat foods began to crowd grocery store shelves.

What happened next? For one thing, dieters became dependent on low-fat foods that were still highly processed and in many instances, full of artificial ingredients and chemicals. For another, even people who avoided these fake foods in lieu of natural high-carbohydrate diets full of whole grains still either gained weight or found their blood sugar rocketing up and plummeting down again.

As more medical studies were conducted, it became apparent that limiting fat wasn't the solution after all, nor was eating unlimited amounts of carbohydrates. It wasn't until the last decade or so that researchers, doctors, and nutritionists began to discover that a high-carbohydrate, low-fat diet wasn't all it was cracked up to be.

First of all, carbohydrates in the human diet are best when they come from natural sources and are as unrefined as possible—the natural foods movement in the late 20th Century got that part right.

Second, the consumption of carbohydrates has to be balanced with a reasonable intake of both protein and fat. Yes, fat was back on the "good" list, but recent research had made some new discoveries. Not all fats are created equal. Many types of fat that were thought to be dangerous, like those in butter or avocados, are actually good for you. Conversely, many that were advocated as healthy, like the trans fats in margarine, were found to raise cholesterol and promote the risk of heart disease. As you can imagine, those fats are now on the "bad" list.

How does this all relate to the Atkins diet, you ask? For starters, the research about the benefits of eating fats and limiting carbohydrates, like on the Atkins diet, were validated. More people in the healthcare community have gotten behind the Atkins diet as a medically sound way to lose or maintain weight.

Additionally, virtually everyone now knows the virtues of eating natural foods versus processed ones, and the Atkins diet today reflects that. Instead of suggesting foods that are largely artificial to satisfy cravings for sugar and starch, the Atkins diet recommends creating low-carb versions of favorite no-nos from natural ingredients. Manufactured products that are marketed under the Atkins name are made with fewer artificial elements to make them more like homemade Atkins-friendly dishes.

Other ways the Atkins diet has been updated include:

- introduction of the Atkins 20 and Atkins 40 plans, two pathways that permit 20 and 40 grams of net carbohydrates per day, respectively (used to be just 20 grams)

- focus on good fats as sources for fat content in the diet

- reduction in the total daily percentage of protein

- emphasis on fruits and vegetables as carbohydrate sources instead of bread, grain products, and processed low-carb foods (more vitamins and fiber)

- broader range of healthy carbohydrate options when

dieters are ready to add them back to their diets

- coffee allowed at all stages of the diet, as well as some alcohol during later stages

- some dairy now allowed during the induction phase, whereas before it was prohibited

- ability to remain at any stage of the diet for as long as is needed

- net carbs more important than total carbs (net carbs = total carbs – fiber)

CHAPTER 4

Benefits of the Atkins Diet

If the Atkins diet is sounding more and more appealing as you read this, great! You may have to make a case for the diet, though, to your significant other or coworkers, who will certainly notice the change in your eating habits. Let's review the benefits you've learned so far, as well as talk about a few you may not know about yet.

Rapid Results

One reason so many people like the Atkins diet is that it generally yields results fast. This is a great boon if you have a lot of weight to lose or followed diets in the past where you went months without seeing the scale go down. Seeing weight loss almost immediately can be a fantastic motivator when it comes to sticking with a diet.

If you follow the diet properly, you should continue to lose weight at a steady rate until you reach your goal weight. (There are tips, however, in Chapter 15, should you hit a weight loss plateau.)

Diet Longevity

The Atkins diet isn't so much a diet as it is a lifestyle change. While you can start Atkins 40 even if you just have a few pounds to lose, you can progress to later stages of the diet when you reach your goal weight. What's the advantage of staying on the diet? First and foremost, you won't gain back all the weight you just lost. Diet yo-yoing is one of the biggest reasons people ultimately give up on trying to manage their weight altogether.

When you remain on the Atkins diet long term, you know

you're filling your body with healthy foods and staying away from things it doesn't need, like refined starches and sugars. You'll always be eating a proper balance of carbohydrates, protein, and fat, and you'll know you're following a diet that's medically sound.

No More Ups and Downs

With the Atkins diet, gone are the days of intense food cravings that lead to binging on unhealthy junk, followed by feeling guilty about your dietary transgressions. Once you make it through the induction stage of the diet, you'll have gotten rid of longing for food that doesn't benefit you, especially sugar.

When you eliminate sugar and excess starch from your diet, you get your blood sugar and insulin levels under control. This means no more of those unpleasant roller coaster rides where you're all amped up at first and crashing and burning a few hours later.

Not only is eliminating ups and downs better for your weight and your overall health, it's better for your mood too. Food-related mood swings will be a thing of the past on the Atkins diet.

Ease of Use

As mentioned earlier, and as you'll learn in greater detail as you read on, the new Atkins diet is very user friendly. You can start the diet where you need to with respect to both your weight goals and your personal health. You can stay in any one phase for as long as you need to. And when you're ready to make a change to your diet, the Atkins systems offers clear-cut steps as to how to do it—which foods you can add back to your diet and in what quantities.

Once you're done with this book, you'll know which foods are gone from your diet forever, which ones are just absent temporarily, and which elements you can eat at any phase of the diet. Because of how popular the Atkins diet is, you'll also be able to stay on the diet when you want to cook your favorite foods or eat out at a restaurant. There are numerous substitutions for foods that aren't included on the diet, so you won't feel deprived, even in the earlier, more limited induction phase. Many restaurants now offer Atkins options on their menus, and there are a wealth of Atkins-friendly recipes online for you to make at home.

Extended Health Benefits

One of the advantages of all the recent research into low-carbohydrate, high-fat diets is that other health benefits of these diets have been revealed. In many instances, triglyceride levels, part of one's total cholesterol, are actually reduced in people who follow the Atkins diet, in spite of its high fat content. And even in instances where LDL (low-density lipoprotein), the so-called "bad" cholesterol, is raised on the Atkins diet, researchers are finding that the size of the LDL particles is larger. Larger LDL particles are preferable as they don't build up and clog arteries the way smaller ones do.

It is now well known that eliminating unstable blood sugar is both desirable and a benefit of the Atkins diet. Some patients with diabetes are able to reduce or discontinue their medications while on the Atkins diet (never do this without consulting your healthcare provider first, though).

Many people on a common Western diet today may not have full-blown diabetes, but they have insulin resistance. This is a condition where the body doesn't respond to insulin, the hormone that helps metabolize carbohydrates, as it should. The consequences of insulin resistance include weight gain and roller coastering blood sugar. In some instances, it can lead to clinical diabetes.

It is believed that many people have insulin resistance and

don't even know it. It is also postulated that insulin resistance is responsible for many of the high-carbohydrate diet problems described in Chapter 3. The Atkins diet can reduce or eliminate insulin resistance by getting rid of the body's need to produce so much insulin through a low-carbohydrate diet.

Further research shows that low-carbohydrate diets, like Atkins, can also reduce the risk of metabolic syndrome. This condition is a combination of high blood pressure, high blood sugar, high cholesterol, and weight gain (particularly around the torso) that can be a precursor to diabetes. People with metabolic syndrome are also at risk for cardiac and peripheral vascular disease.

High-fat, low-sugar diets are beneficial for the skin as well. The good fats in the diet nourish the skin from the inside out, and the elimination of sugar prevents glycation, a process by which skin is aged prematurely or can become inflamed and break out.

Chronic pain patients tend to do well on the Atkins diet as well. In addition to helping degenerative joint disease, like arthritis, through weight loss, a high-fat, low carbohydrate diet can reduce overall bodily inflammation.

Ongoing pain from conditions like diabetic neuropathy and multiple sclerosis may also respond to being in ketosis, as this pain responds to anticonvulsant medications. Anticonvulsant medications for epilepsy patients, as you may recall, can sometimes be replaced by a ketogenic diet, like the induction phase of Atkins 20.

For the same reason, researchers are now postulating that bipolar disorder, which is also treated with anti-seizure medications, may respond to a low-carbohydrate, high-fat diet that keeps the patient in ketosis. This is a current area of clinical study, along with similar diets to control thyroid disorders and even cancer.

The Atkins Diet - 17

CHAPTER 5

Misconceptions About the Atkins Diet

If your family, friends, and colleagues aren't completely sold on the idea of the Atkins diet, you may hear some of the following misconceptions about it. Here are some facts to counter their misinformation.

Wrong: The Atkins diet is not medically sound.

Right: The Atkins diet, along with other similar low-carbohydrate, high-fat diets, has been studied in reputable clinical trials. When properly followed, and not undertaken against medical advice, the Atkins diet is safe enough to stay on for life. Recent studies have vindicated the Atkins diet, which was initially criticized when it was thought fat was bad.

Wrong: The Atkins diet is just a temporary diet

Right: The Atkins diet is best used as a permanent lifestyle change, not a quick fix to lose a few pounds. Because the diet offers so many options to suit a variety of needs, people who stay on Atkins even when they don't need to lose weight are basically just following a healthy, low-carbohydrate eating plan.

Wrong: You can eat as much as you want on the Atkins diet.

Right: You can eat as much as you want of certain foods, but total calories still matter on the Atkins diet. You calculate how many calories you need to consume to lose or gain weight or to stay the same, based on your size, age, activity level, etc. Once you know how many calories you need, the

Atkins diet tells you how many grams of each food to eat. The basic metabolic equations still apply:

- If you eat more calories than you burn, you will gain weight.

- If you eat fewer calories than you burn, you will lose weight.

- If you burn the equivalent of what you eat in calories, your weight will remain the same.

Wrong: You can't be a vegetarian or follow a religious diet on the Atkins diet.

Right: You can certainly maintain a vegetarian diet on the Atkins plan. It may be a little more challenging, and you'll have fewer options, but that's true of regular vegetarian eating outside the Atkins diet too. You will be able to consume foods like dairy, eggs, and legumes to obtain adequate protein that other dieters get by eating meat.

You can also follow the Atkins diet and still maintain a halal or kosher diet by eliminating foods that you are not permitted to eat (pork products or shellfish), buying special versions of the same foods (kosher or halal meats), and combining foods in ways that don't violate your dietary rules.

Wrong: The Atkins diet is only for the obese.

Right: Almost anyone can benefit from the Atkins diet. While it's a wonderful weight loss plan for someone who is obese and wants to lose a great deal of weight, it's also great for someone with just 10 pounds to lose or who wants to keep carbohydrates in check for life.

There are, however, a few groups of people who should NOT follow the Atkins diet, and these include:

- people who have gall bladder disease or have had their gall bladders removed

- people with serious kidney disease or history of kidney failure

- people with liver disease

- people with metabolic disorders or who cannot digest fats

- people who have had gastric bypass/bariatric surgery

- people with a history of pancreatitis

- people with a history of eating disorders

- some pregnant or lactating women (some may be able to do Atkins 40)

If you're not sure if the Atkins diet is safe for you, consult your healthcare provider or a professional nutritionist.

CHAPTER 6

The Structure of the Atkins Diet

The Atkins diet has two basic pathways or plans: Atkins 20 and Atkins 40. Atkins 20 starts dieters out with a limit of 20 grams of net carbohydrates per day, whereas Atkins 40 allows 40 grams per day. Remember, net carbs are equal to your total carbs minus fiber.

How do you know which plan to choose? Atkins 20 is more restrictive and is closer to the original version of the Atkins diet. It is recommended for the following situations:

- if you have more than 40 pounds to lose

- if you are diabetic or pre-diabetic

- if you are a woman with a waist larger than 35 inches

- if you are a man with a waist larger than 40 inches

- if you are looking for a ketogenic diet, where ketones from fat, rather than glucose, are your primary energy source

Atkins 40 is a newer version of the diet. If you fit any of the following criteria, Atkins 40 is the way to go:

- if you have less than 40 pounds to lose

- if you think staying on the Atkins 20 plan would be difficult enough that you would wind up quitting the diet

- if you are vegetarian and require a larger variety of foods to choose from to replace meat

- if you are pregnant or breastfeeding (with your physician's permission)

Both the Atkins 20 and the Atkins 40 plans allow dieters to start with three servings of protein per day, with each serving equal to four to six ounces. Both plans also allow three servings of additional healthy fats per day. What are considered healthy fats? These are foods like olive oil and butter on the Atkins diet.

Where the Atkins 20 and the Atkins 40 plans differ is in carbohydrate intake. The Atkins 20 plan limits the sources of your carbohydrates to leafy greens, low-carb vegetables, and high-fat dairy foods like sour cream and hard cheeses.

The Atkins 40 plan, in contrast, gives you a broader range of carbohydrates to choose from. On Atkins 40, about one-third of your carbohydrates should come from vegetables. The remainder of your carbs can be derived from whole grains, nuts, and fruits.

The Atkins 20 and Atkins 40 plans also differ when it comes to adding foods back into your diet after the induction phase. Usually dieters who are trying to lose weight start returning previously off-limits foods once they get within about 10-15 pounds of their goal weight. (If you are following the Atkins diet for reasons other than weight loss, take a look at your personal goals when deciding at which phase to begin the diet. It may be the induction phase, or it may be later in the diet.)

On Atkins 20, you add carbohydrates back to your diet in increments of five grams; the Atkins 40 plan suggests adding 10 grams at a time. While 10-gram increases are made about once per week on the Atkins 40 plan, your progress may be slower on Atkins 20. The Atkins 40 plan lets you add carbohydrates from any source on the allowed foods list, whereas the Atkins 20 plan uses a "carb ladder" to slowly add different types of carbohydrates back to the diet.

The carbohydrate ladder on **Atkins 20** (first foods added to last foods) looks like this:

- seeds and nuts

- berries, cherries, and all melons except watermelon

- fresh cheeses, like cottage cheese and ricotta, and yogurt made from whole milk

- legumes, such as lentils, chick peas, and beans

- tomato juice, vegetable juice blends, and fruits

- high-carbohydrate vegetables, such as acorn squash and root vegetables

Finally, the Atkins 20 plan suggests taking a bit more time and care when adding any last foods once you reach the lifetime maintenance phase, where you have hit your goal weight and want to stay there. The plan recommends still adding foods one at a time, and it is advisable to keep notes as you return elements to your diet. This way, if any food triggers any sensitivities or causes you to gain back weight, you'll know what the culprit is right away and can eliminate it from your diet permanently.

This Atkins 20 strategy is also ideal for people who don't necessarily have a lot of weight to lose but may feel certain foods cause symptoms of discomfort or cause their weight to increase rapidly. If this describes you, consider starting with the Atkins 40 plan when it comes to the amount of net carbohydrates you can consume but using the Atkins 20 method of adding new foods more carefully.

Technically, the Atkins diet has four phases:

1. the **Induction Phase** to kick-off your diet and

immediately start losing weight

2. the **Balancing Phase**, where you slowly add more low-carb elements to your diet

3. the **Fine-tuning Phase**, during which you are adding more foods as you approach your goal weight

4. the **Maintenance Phase**, where you have determined the best diet to keep your weight where you want it and keep food sensitivities at bay

As alluded to earlier in this book, however, people follow the Atkins diet for a variety of reasons, and everyone's metabolism and general health is different. You may find yourself skipping the induction phase or staying in it forever, or you may take longer to add foods back to your diet. While many people respond well to a highly structured diet, others do better when they can adjust the parameters to their personal needs, and the Atkins diet allows for both approaches to dieting.

Are you worried about keeping track of your net carbs, your calories, and the foods you are allowed to eat at the various stages of the Atkins diet? Never fear, adhering to the Atkins diet has never been easier with the tools available on the Internet today. You can find numerous websites online where you can enter all your information to get the calculations you need, and you can download apps for your mobile devices as well. These programs allow you to re-enter data as your weight loss or other health goals change, so you'll always know what you can and cannot eat.

CHAPTER 7

Starting the Atkins Diet

Now that you know a little more about the different pathways and options on the Atkins diet, it's time to learn about starting the diet. The subtitle of this book is *"Set Yourself Up for Success,"* and by doing a little work in preparation for the Atkins diet, you can do just that.

First, it bears reminding again that if you have any doubts about whether the Atkins diet is safe for you, you should consult a professional healthcare provider before starting. Once you have the all-clear, start thinking about the best time to begin your diet.

The induction phase of the Atkins diet can be challenging for some folks, and you may not feel well for a week or so while your metabolism is shifting. You will have cravings for starch and sugar for a few days, which may make you irritable. You may experience a reduction in your energy level. You will likely have changes in one direction or another to your gastric motility and may need to visit the restroom more frequently. You will also be thirstier than normal and may have dry eyes.

If you start the program at Atkins 20, you will likely be in ketosis after a few days. The early phase of any ketogenic diet can be challenging; in fact some people call the symptoms described above the "keto flu."

Therefore, try to plan the start of your Atkins diet for a time when you can rest, relax, and take care of yourself, such as over a weekend, when you don't have to work. Plan to take a few days off your workout routine too as you likely won't feel up to it.

Many dieters find it helpful to establish a support network before undertaking a big lifestyle change like starting the Atkins diet. Whether that means dieting with your significant other, finding another diet buddy, or joining an online forum, you may feel better if you have someone to talk to about what you're going through.

In addition to getting your pantry ready for the Atkins diet, which is discussed in the two following chapters, here are some other things you should do:

- Invest in a high-quality water bottle or two. You'll be drinking a lot more water on the Atkins diet than in the past.

- Make sure you have some salt in the house. When you eat carbohydrates, you are helping your body retain hydration, but when you eliminate carbs from your diet, you need more salt to keep from excreting too much water as urine and sweat. You will also lose some salt (sodium) by urinating more frequently on the Atkins diet. You need sodium to help regulate all the cells in your body. You don't want to become hyponatremic, which is the medical term for being too low in sodium.

- Buy a good multivitamin tablet, if you don't take one already, as well as potassium and magnesium supplements. While you will get many good nutrients through your diet, you may not get the daily requirements for each. You'll feel better if you get all the vitamins and minerals you need each day.

- Purchase some small portable food containers or compartmentalized boxes for bringing food with you. While there are plenty of places where you'll find Atkins-friendly food, you may encounter situations where there is nothing you can eat without breaking your diet. Instead of falling off the wagon, get in the habit of carrying some Atkins-friendly food with you. (See Chapter 13 for suggestions.)

- If you don't keep your schedule or save recipes on a mobile device, buy a calendar and a binder with loose paper and plastic sheet protectors. The calendar will help you keep track of your Atkins diet phases and weight loss goals. You can use the binder to write down notes, hold meal plans, and collect recipes printed off the Internet or torn from magazines. The more variety you can offer yourself, the more you will be likely to stick to your diet.

CHAPTER 8

Foods to Which You Will Bid Farewell

There will be foods that you can no longer eat on the Atkins diet, either temporarily or permanently. Nonperishable foods you are likely to reintroduce to your diet soon can be kept, but those that you intend to ban for good should be eliminated from your household if possible.

If others in your home aren't participating in the Atkins diet, you may have to simply sequester these unacceptable foods, so they're not constantly tempting you. Otherwise, take them to the office for your coworkers, give them to your neighbors, or donate them to a local food bank.

Foods you will not be able to eat at all during any phase of the Atkins diet include:

- white flour or products made with white flour (breads, pasta, pastries, and desserts)

- white rice

- sugar and products made with sugar (candy, cookies, etc.)

- highly processed and artificial foods, including "low-fat" and "diet" foods

- trans fats (hint: look for the word "hydrogenated" on the label)

- certain vegetable oils (including cottonseed oil and canola oil)

As you have already read, you may be able to add certain other foods back into your diet, depending on your personal

28 - The Atkins Diet

metabolism and activity level. "Iffy" foods include items like potatoes, yams, autumn squashes, legumes, and higher carbohydrate fruits like apples and cherries.

Additionally, things like alcohol and some dairy may be omitted during the induction phase of the Atkins diet, but they may be added back during subsequent phases of the plan. These temporary omissions are so you can get into maximum fat-burning mode faster and also so you can test for food sensitivities once you try adding them back to your diet.

Food sensitivities can manifest as more than just an allergic-type reaction or digestive upset. For some folks, eating certain foods stalls their metabolism. You don't want to keep eating something that keeps you from losing weight until you are in the maintenance phase.

CHAPTER 9

Shopping for the Atkins Diet

While you will be able to broaden your menu as you progress through the different phases of the Atkins diet, most people start with the induction phase, which limits their grocery list for a few weeks. To get you started, here is a handy shopping list you can use to stock up your pantry, so you're ready to go. Try to find the best quality or organic versions of these items whenever possible.

Meat and Poultry

- steak
- ground beef
- beef or pork roasts, ribs and chops
- veal
- lamb
- ham and Canadian bacon
- sausage
- bacon
- prosciutto
- salami and deli cold cuts
- jerky
- eggs
- chicken
- turkey
- duck and goose
- quail and pheasant
- Cornish game hen
- ostrich
- venison and other game
- bison or buffalo
- other _____

30 - The Atkins Diet

FISH and SEAFOOD (SHELLFISH)

- fish filets and steaks, like salmon, tilapia, halibut, flounder, trout, sole, cod, and mackerel

- canned and fresh tuna

- sardines and anchovies

- herring

- lobster and crab

- squid and octopus

- shellfish: scallops, shrimp, oysters, clams, and mussels

- other _____

Dairy Products (depending on your induction diet)

- butter
- full-fat, heavy cream
- sour cream
- Greek yogurt
- cheeses _____
- other _____

Nuts and Seeds (depending on your plan)

- walnuts

- pecans

- almonds

- hazelnuts (filberts)

- pistachios

- macadamias

- flax seeds

- sesame seeds

- sunflower seeds

- pumpkin seeds

- chia seeds
- nut butters _____
- other _____

Vegetables and Fruits

- avocados
- broccoli, broccoli rabe, and cauliflower
- mushrooms
- bell peppers
- asparagus
- eggplant
- green beans
- spinach, kale, collard greens, and Swiss chard
- leaf lettuce, arugula, and escarole
- alfalfa sprouts
- endive, fennel, and celery
- radishes and daikon
- kohlrabi
- jicama
- rhubarb
- okra
- snow peas
- water chestnuts
- cucumbers
- cabbage, sauerkraut, and bok choy
- Brussels sprouts
- artichokes, artichoke hearts and hearts of palm
- bamboo shoots
- pumpkin, spaghetti squash, zucchini, and summer squash
- leeks, scallions, and chives
- garlic

- fresh herbs _____

Other Items

- oils: coconut, soybean, grapeseed, walnt, olive, sunflower, safflower, and sesame

- ghee (clarified butter, frequently used in Indian cooking)

- tallow/lard/duck fat

- olives

- dill pickles

- tamari (wheat-free soy sauce)

- other _____

- full-fat, low-carb salad dressings

- unsweetened cocoa powder

- stevia

- spices _____

- ranch seasoning

- unsweetened soy milk

- mayonnaise

- mustard

- hot sauce

- other _____

The Atkins Diet - 33

CHAPTER 10

A Typical Daily Menu on Atkins

Now that you know more about how the Atkins diet works and what's entailed in starting it, let's look at a typical day on the diet. It's all well and good to have a list of acceptable foods, but how are you going to put them together to create a fun, tasty menu for yourself?

There are thousands of ways you can combine foods on the Atkins diet to get the nutrients you need with the variety you crave and still stay within the correct fat/protein/carbohydrate ratios and caloric limitations. Here are some ideas, so you can see what an average daily menu on Atkins looks like. Some selections are from the induction phase, so remember that you'll be able to add in things like more dairy, wine, and slighter higher carbohydrate vegetables as you move into the other phases of the diet.

Breakfast Options

- spinach and mushroom omelet, cooked in butter

- bacon and eggs

- crustless quiche, using ham or bacon on the outside

- frittata with eggs, vegetables, and ham, bacon, or sausage

- eggs in avocado halves

- eggs with lox or smoked fish

- cottage cheese with fruit and slivered almonds

- Greek yogurt with fruit and chia seeds

- protein shake

- cheesecake pancakes made with cream cheese

Lunch Options

- chicken stir fry with broccoli or snow peas and red bell peppers

- salad topped with grilled shrimp

- breadless BLT inside romaine lettuce

- zucchini boats stuffed with sausage

- eggplant or Portobello mushroom pizza

- salmon- or crab-stuffed avocado

- egg salad lettuce wraps

- dinner leftovers from the night before

Dinner Options

- steak with butter and asparagus

- grilled chicken and caprese salad

- baked eggplant casserole

- Chinese restaurant-style chicken lettuce wraps

- bacon-wrapped shrimp with a crispy slaw salad

- bunless cheeseburger with veggies

- baked cod with zucchini "tater" tots

- chili with cheese and sour cream

- roast pork loin or chops with cauliflower mash

- cheesy taco skillet (no shells)

- steamed lobster and artichokes dipped in melted butter and lemon juice

- Atkins-adapted chopped salad or Niçoise salad

Snack and Dessert Options

- sugar-free Jello

- nuts

- sugar-free Popsicles

- pickles

- hard boiled eggs

- cheese sticks

- berries

- olives

- sour cream cupcakes

- coffee frappe

- coconut custard

If these selections sound appealing, be sure to check out Chapter 12 for some Atkins diet recipes you can try at home, as well as tips for taking your diet on the go. You'll get advice for what to include when you pack your own snacks and lunches and how to substitute Atkins-approved dishes for some of your old favorites.

CHAPTER 11

Beverages on Atkins

Let's take a moment here to talk more about beverages on the Atkins Diet. You may not believe it, but what you drink can have as many, if not more, calories than what you eat if you're not careful. Therefore, it's imperative that you select your beverages on the Atkins diet with care.

Of course, water should be your number one beverage all day, every day. Water provides many benefits to your diet and your health:

- It helps you digest your food better.

- It keeps you from being constipated.

- It helps flush waste and toxins from your body, including fat you are burning.

- It keeps your muscles and connective tissue operating at top condition.

- It participates in your joint lubrication.

- It improves the function of your cardiovascular and respiratory systems.

- It helps prevent fatigue and "brain fog."

- It helps process dehydrating beverages, such as coffee, caffeinated tea, caffeinated diet soda, and alcohol.

- It replenishes fluid lost during sweat, especially if you work out.

- It makes your skin and hair look and feel better.

- It helps fill you up, so you aren't tempted to cheat on your diet.

If you have trouble remembering to drink water, keep a pitcher on your desk at work, take a water bottle with you in the car, and bring a water bottle to the gym or yoga studio. If water bores you, try adding fresh mint leaves, lemon slices, or cucumber slices for flavor and freshness.

Providing you are getting adequate water, however, the Atkins diet does let you drink other beverages within the scope of your total daily caloric intake.

Beverages permitted on the Atkins diet include:

- diet soda and diet mixers, like tonic water

- coffee

- tea

- unsweetened almond and soy milk

- milk (sometimes omitted during the induction phase, especially if sensitivity to lactose, the sugar in milk, is suspected)

- dry white and red wine (after the induction phase)

- unflavored spirits, like vodka, whiskey, brandy, rum, tequila, and gin (after the induction phase)

Note that fruit juices, sugared sodas and mixers, flavored spirits that may contain sugar, and beer, which is essentially bread in a bottle, are not permitted on the Atkins diet.

If you drink your coffee black, no problem. If you like it black with sugar, substitute stevia for the sugar. You can also enjoy sugar-free flavored syrups in your coffee during all phases of the Atkins diet, and serve any coffee drink over ice or mixed with ice in the blender to make a frappe.

Depending on whether or not you are withholding dairy, you may or may not be able to drink coffee with milk. However, once you reach that level, you may be pleased to know you can drink your coffee with heavy cream, instead of skim milk, as this is actually lower in carbohydrates and preferable on the Atkins diet. Just be sure you don't use whipped cream that has been prepared with sugar, which is how some places serve it.

Want to feel like you're getting a rich coffee drink from one of those pricey coffee shops? Here's a recipe that won't break the bank or your diet rules:

1. Crush 2 cups ice in a blender

2. Add 2 scoops of vanilla protein shake mix, 3 tablespoons heavy cream, 3 tablespoons sugar-free flavored coffee syrup (hazelnut or vanilla), and ¼ cup of chilled, strong coffee (you can chill what's left in the pot when you brew hot coffee).

3. Blend on high until well mixed. You may want to wait until the last few seconds to add the cream for a thicker consistency.

When consuming alcohol, try to alternate one glass of water between every alcoholic beverage. Be aware that you may become inebriated faster on the Atkins diet, without all those carbs to slow down the absorption of alcohol. Hangovers can be worse too, so be sure you don't overindulge at the bar.

It's smart to drink at least one extra glass of water for every caffeinated beverage you consume too. Your body needs water to process the caffeine, and you may experience a diuretic effect when you drink caffeinated beverages. Don't wait until you're thirsty to drink that water; just chase your caffeine with a big tumbler of good old H2O.

CHAPTER 12

Sample Recipes for the Atkins Diet

Cheesecake Pancakes

Going without bread and baked goods can be tough on the Atkins diet, but there are ways you can fake it with recipes that don't contain glucose but taste like they do. Cream cheese-based pancakes are a low-carb diet staple, and they're a perfect alternative to dishes where the eggs are front and center, like in many Atkins recipes. This gluten-free pancake alternative won't leave you sleepy and wanting to go back to bed right after breakfast either.

1. Blend 2 eggs, 2 ounces of cream cheese, 1 packet of stevia, and ½ teaspoon cinnamon in a blender.

2. Let the mixture rest for a few minutes. You want all the bubbles to disperse before cooking it.

3. Ladle about ¼ of the batter onto a hot griddle greased with butter.

4. Fry until golden (about 2 minutes). Then, flip the pancakes and cook the other side.

5. Serve with sugar-free syrup or fresh berries.

Caprese Salad

This is a recipe you can use when you add tomatoes back into your diet (most folks omit them during the induction phase of Atkins). The caprese salad is a southern Italian classic, and it's a perfect recipe to have in your Atkins diet toolbox. The caprese salad has numerous things going for it, besides being Atkins-friendly:

with ice in the blender to make a frappe.

Depending on whether or not you are withholding dairy, you may or may not be able to drink coffee with milk. However, once you reach that level, you may be pleased to know you can drink your coffee with heavy cream, instead of skim milk, as this is actually lower in carbohydrates and preferable on the Atkins diet. Just be sure you don't use whipped cream that has been prepared with sugar, which is how some places serve it.

Want to feel like you're getting a rich coffee drink from one of those pricey coffee shops? Here's a recipe that won't break the bank or your diet rules:

1. Crush 2 cups ice in a blender

2. Add 2 scoops of vanilla protein shake mix, 3 tablespoons heavy cream, 3 tablespoons sugar-free flavored coffee syrup (hazelnut or vanilla), and ¼ cup of chilled, strong coffee (you can chill what's left in the pot when you brew hot coffee).

3. Blend on high until well mixed. You may want to wait until the last few seconds to add the cream for a thicker consistency.

When consuming alcohol, try to alternate one glass of water between every alcoholic beverage. Be aware that you may become inebriated faster on the Atkins diet, without all those carbs to slow down the absorption of alcohol. Hangovers can be worse too, so be sure you don't overindulge at the bar.

It's smart to drink at least one extra glass of water for every caffeinated beverage you consume too. Your body needs water to process the caffeine, and you may experience a diuretic effect when you drink caffeinated beverages. Don't wait until you're thirsty to drink that water; just chase your caffeine with a big tumbler of good old H2O.

CHAPTER 12

Sample Recipes for the Atkins Diet

Cheesecake Pancakes

Going without bread and baked goods can be tough on the Atkins diet, but there are ways you can fake it with recipes that don't contain glucose but taste like they do. Cream cheese-based pancakes are a low-carb diet staple, and they're a perfect alternative to dishes where the eggs are front and center, like in many Atkins recipes. This gluten-free pancake alternative won't leave you sleepy and wanting to go back to bed right after breakfast either.

1. Blend 2 eggs, 2 ounces of cream cheese, 1 packet of stevia, and ½ teaspoon cinnamon in a blender.

2. Let the mixture rest for a few minutes. You want all the bubbles to disperse before cooking it.

3. Ladle about ¼ of the batter onto a hot griddle greased with butter.

4. Fry until golden (about 2 minutes). Then, flip the pancakes and cook the other side.

5. Serve with sugar-free syrup or fresh berries.

Caprese Salad

This is a recipe you can use when you add tomatoes back into your diet (most folks omit them during the induction phase of Atkins). The caprese salad is a southern Italian classic, and it's a perfect recipe to have in your Atkins diet toolbox. The caprese salad has numerous things going for it, besides being Atkins-friendly:

1. It only takes a few minutes to make.

2. It requires only three ingredients, plus the dressing, which you can make yourself in a jiffy.

3. It travels easily for a lunch or snack on the go.

4. It can be a main course for lunch or a side course with dinner.

5. It can be an appetizer for a crowd when you have company or when you're invited to someone else's house.

6. It can be stuffed inside chicken or fish and eaten warm for a more gourmet feel or a change of pace.

The caprese salad should be assembled just before it is served. If you're taking it on the road with you, keep the ingredients in separate compartments, and hold the dressing on the side until you're ready to eat. For a simple, beautiful presentation that sings of summer on the Mediterranean, serve your caprese salad on a plain white plate, so the colors and the dressing really pop.

1. Cut the best beefsteak tomatoes you can find into ¼-inch slices.

2. Slice fresh buffalo mozzarella cheese balls into ¼-inch slices.

3. Lay the tomatoes and mozzarella cheese in horizontal layers on a plate with whole basil leaves between each layer.

4. Sprinkle with a pinch of sea salt and fresh-ground black pepper.

5. Drizzle with extra virgin olive oil and high-quality balsamic vinegar.

Chili

Having a chile recipe that complies with your Atkins diet means you'll always have something the whole family can eat and a dish you can take to potlucks or Superbowl Sunday parties. This is an easy chili recipe to get you started, but it tastes rich with its layers of spices and cheese on top. You can easily adapt this recipe too for preparation in a slow cooker, or you can put it in the crock pot on low once it's done so people can help themselves all day long.

1. In a deep skillet or heavy saucepan, heat 1 tablespoon extra virgin olive oil over medium-high heat. Add 2 chopped jalapeño peppers and 1 teaspoon of garlic. Cook for just half a minute until fragrant.

2. Add 2 pounds ground beef.

3. Add the following spices:

    o ½ teaspoon salt

    o ¼ teaspoon cayenne pepper

    o 2 tablespoons chili powder

    o 1-1/2 teaspoons ground cumin

    o 1/8 teaspoon cinnamon

4. Stir and cook until the beef is browned. Drain off any excess grease.

5. Add 14 cans diced tomatoes (14.5 ounce size) with liquid.

6. Bring mixture to a boil, and then reduce to a simmer until ready to serve.

7. Garnish with grated cheddar or Monterey jack cheese and a dollop of sour cream.

CHAPTER 13

Eating Your Favorite Foods on the Atkins Diet and Dining Out

Just because you aren't eating white flour and sugar anymore doesn't mean you have to give up all your favorite foods. Hopefully, after reading some of the food ideas and recipes in the previous sections, you're starting to realize how possible it is to stick to the Atkins diet and still eat satisfying, delicious meals.

If you look online or purchase an Atkins cookbook, you'll find many more recipes you love, including ways to prepare muffins and desserts with substitutes for flour and sugar. Here are some other substitutions you can make, whether you're dining out or eating in, and many of these are already on the menu at your best-loved restaurants.

Old Favorite	Atkins-Friendly Version
Quiche	Crustless quiche with ham or bacon
Tacos	Tacos wrapped in lettuce or taco skillet
Nachos	Pork rind nachos or nacho skillet
Pizza	Eggplant or Portobello mushroom pizza
Sandwiches	Lettuce wraps
Tater tots	Zucchini tots
Pasta	Spaghetti squash noodles
Mashed potatoes	Cauliflower mash
Cheeseburger	Bunless burger or wrapped in lettuce

Chips	Fried veggie or parmesan cheese crisps
Sloppy joes	Bunless sloppy joe in lettuce or bowl
Chinese takeout	Chicken stir fry or lettuce wraps
Ice cream	Sugar-free ice cream or custard
Candy bars	Dark, high-cocoa content chocolate

If you're dining at a gourmet or specialty restaurant, many dishes are made to order, so you may be able to order off the menu to get an Atkins-friendly version. For example, if a restaurant normally serves mashed potatoes with all their steaks and chops, ask if you can substitute mashed cauliflower or an extra serving of asparagus instead. If there's nothing on the dessert cart that you're allowed to eat, see if the chef can prepare a bowl of berries in heavy cream instead.

Dining at someone else's home might be a bit tougher. If you know the host well, simply ask if you can bring along something that complies with your diet (you'll learn to love potlucks on Atkins) or if they can hold off on any sauces and the like when serving your meat and vegetables.

When attending formal events, like work banquets or weddings, see if you can phone the caterer in advance to inquire about the menu ingredients. Usually, they'll have several requests for special meals for people on various diets, such as for diabetes or gluten intolerance. Ask if they can offer you an Atkins-friendly version of whatever they're serving, and you're likely to get it.

Special meals these days on airlines are a crap shoot. If you're not sure if an airline will have anything you can eat, bring your own containers of food. It's a good idea in general on Atkins to keep a little cooler of foods you can eat with you on the road, whenever you think there might not be Atkinscompliant dishes available. Here are some suggestions for foods you can carry with you with ease. Just think twice about bringing nut products or anything too aromatic on an airplane, in consideration of your seatmates.

- chunks
- of meat, poultry, or ham
- sliced sausage or salami
- prosciutto or deli meats
- lettuce wraps
- bacon strips
- sardines or chunks of tuna or salmon
- boiled eggs
- avocado halves
- nuts
- pumpkin or sunflower seeds
- cheese sticks, cubes of cheese, or mozzarella balls
- beef or venison jerky
- olives
- tomato wedges
- cucumber slices
- slices of bell pepper
- snow peas
- radishes
- celery sticks with sugar-free peanut butter
- asparagus spears
- berries
- Greek yogurt
- low-carb dressings and dips
- squares of high-cocoa content chocolate
- sugar-free desserts

CHAPTER 14

Tips for Staying on the Atkins Diet

Staying on the Atkins diet can take some willpower and focus. During the early phases, you're still getting used to the acceptable foods list and perhaps making a metabolic shift to ketogenesis if you follow the Atkins 20 plan. The longer you are on any diet, the easier it is to get bored with it or be tempted to cheat.

Whether you're in the induction phase of the Atkins diet or years into your maintenance phase, here are some tips to help keep you on track.

Don't skip meals. When you first start a diet, you may think it will speed up your weight loss to skip a meal here and there. Once you're used to your diet, you may be less focused on it—kind of like the process of learning to drive—and you may forget to eat sometimes. Skipping meals on the Atkins diet is a no-no because it makes it too easy to binge later, and it's not good for your metabolism. During your waking hours, you shouldn't go longer than six hours without eating on Atkins.

Don't eat foods known to cause you grief. You should find out during the middle phases of the Atkins diet, when you're adding foods back in, if certain items either cause you unpleasant health symptoms or make you gain weight. It can be tough to find out that these are some of your favorite foods or things you've always eaten, but if you want to lose weight and keep it off or banish those unwanted side effects, you'll have to kiss those foods goodbye.

Keep your alcohol consumption in check. Just because alcohol is allowed on the Atkins diet doesn't mean you can go overboard with it. For one thing, it could put your total daily calories over the allowed amount. For another, when you drink alcohol, even though it has no carbohydrates, you are burning the calories from your drink, not burning fat. Alcohol is dehydrating, and staying hydrated is your best friend on the Atkins diet. Finally, everyone knows what alcohol can do to your willpower. Don't let a few too many cocktails undo weeks of great progress.

Drink plenty of water. In case you missed it in the previous paragraph and in other spots in this book, you'll need to drink lots and lots of water on the Atkins diet. If you've not been drinking enough water, all this hydrating may take some getting used to, but it will be good for you in the long run. Not only will you feel better and have an easier time digesting your food without constipation, you'll look better too. Water plumps up the skin and keeps it moist from the inside out, giving it a more youthful appearance. Staying hydrated will make your workouts easier and keep your brain from getting foggy too.

Don't cheat with "just a taste" of something. It can be easy to think that cheating with just a little sugary dessert or a few french fries won't do you any harm. It's just a tiny amount, right? Wrong. The Atkins diet trains your body and your mind to get rid of cravings for empty sugar and starch and for all the nastiness that comes with them. You know how it goes: one minute you're just having a spoon of ice cream, and an hour later you've eaten the whole pint. Don't even tempt yourself.

If you fall off the horse, get back on. Okay, so if you do ignore the paragraph above and eat something you shouldn't, it's not the end of the world. Hopefully, it's not enough to set back your diet in the long-term, but like a sailboat heading for the rocks, the sooner you can correct your course the better. Don't let a little cheating or even a weekend of going off your Atkins diet send you spiraling out of control permanently. Get back into your diet zone as soon as possible, even if it means going back to that induction phase list of foods for a few days to minimize temptation.

Don't give temptation opportunity. Dieting is like other endeavors that require willpower, such as quitting an addiction. Just like someone trying to quit smoking who stays away from bars and other places that trigger the urge to light up, you may need to minimize your exposure to situations that tempt you to go off your diet. If bringing your own Atkins-friendly snacks (see Chapter 13) isn't an option, you may have to figuratively tie yourself to the mast like Odysseus in Homer's *Odyssey* when he wanted to avoid the song of the sirens. Just stay away from office birthday parties, spaghetti suppers, and that table of Girl Scout cookies for sale at the mall. Better yet...

Surround yourself with supportive people. This strategy works with all kinds of challenges, like increasing your wealth, not just dieting. Hang out with people from your gym, join a low-carb cooking club, or start a neighborhood walking group. You'll get positive support, eliminate naysayers, and maybe just pick up some more tips for healthy living along the way.

Exercise. Did you read that part in the last paragraph about going to the gym? While you may not have to join a health club, you should be doing something active or working out regularly. If you exercise with a partner or group of people, you'll be less likely to miss sessions, so try to do at least some of your activities with other folks. Studies show that the most effective way to lose weight is to combine dieting with exercise. You'll see better results with your Atkins diet if you exercise while you're controlling your eating. Building muscle mass also boosts your metabolism even at rest, and you'll get another boost in your fat burning during the hour or so that follows solid aerobic exercise. If spin classes and road running aren't your thing, don't forget that activities like dancing and yard work can get your heart pumping too.

Try new culinary pursuits. Have you ever heard the expression "Familiarity breeds contempt?" In the case of dieting, it might not be contempt exactly, but familiarity can certainly develop into boredom. Medical professionals agree that boredom with a diet is one of the top reasons people fall off the wagon. Don't let it happen to you! One of the best ways to fend off boredom is to keep trying new foods and recipes. With the advent of the Internet, there's no excuse not to find a new Atkins-friendly recipe to try every week. Think too about getting out of your comfort zone and trying some new foods, whether that's a type of vegetable you've never cooked before or some new spices to jazz up your old standbys. Cooking classes are another great way to take your food prep skills to a new level while learning some new recipes.

Create a vision board. If you need a reminder about why you're on the Atkins diet in the first place, why not create a vision board? This is collage of images and motivational sayings to help keep you on track when times get tough. You can use pages torn from magazines and catalogs or an online platform like Pinterest to build a board that's uniquely inspiring for you. You could even do both: have an Internet board that you can take with you on your mobile and another one to plaster on your fridge when you need a little extra help.

CHAPTER 15

Dealing with Weight Loss Plateaus

Sometimes, no matter how hard you seem to working at the Atkins diet, your weight loss might stall for a while. If you experience a weight loss plateau, here are some tips for managing it.

Don't just go by your weight. While weight is usually a good measure of whether you are burning excess fat or not, it's not a 100 percent reliable test. Take a look at how your clothes fit and how your body looks. If you are working out more, it could be that you have gained muscle mass, which weighs more than fat. If your clothing is getting bigger and bigger on you, maybe you don't need to lose any more weight, or maybe you need to let your body catch up to your exercise regimen before it drops any more.

Examine your weight loss goal. Is it possible that the weight loss goal you set for yourself isn't realistic? Perhaps you have always wanted to be a size two or wear a size 38 suit, but it's just not in your genetic makeup. There are all kinds of bodies in the world, but not all of them need to be super skinny to be healthy. If you're not sure whether you should be losing more weight, it may be time to talk to a professional, like a physician, nutritionist or a credentialed personal trainer. Together, you can assess your weight and BMI (body mass index) in the context of your overall build, your age, your medical history, your genetics, etc. Maybe your weight loss goal is closer than you thought; maybe you're already there!

Make sure you're not really overeating. First, double check all your calculations to make certain you're consuming the proper number of calories and net carbs for your weight goals and that you're only eating foods that are on the Atkins "acceptable" list. Next, make sure that what you're eating matches up with those figures. Are you weighing or measuring your food correctly? Or are you just eyeballing amounts and winging it on the calories? Get in the habit of always checking food labels for packaged foods to make sure you're not inadvertently eating more carbohydrates than you thought you were.

Drink more water. Hopefully, you've read that message more than a few times in this book, but it doesn't hurt to hear it again. It's ironic, but drinking more water can actually help you flush unwanted extra fluid from your body. When you drink too little water, your body thinks it's never going to see hydration again, and it hangs onto the water it already has. You can retain this fluid all over your body, and sometimes extra weight can be in the form of water weight. Drinking more water helps regulate your ADH (anti-diuretic hormone) and gets you back to excreting fluid properly. Also, you need water to help flush waste from your body, including all the fat you've been working so hard to burn off.

Make sure you're not consuming anything with aspartame. Clinical trials have shown that the artificial sweetener aspartame is associated with weight gain. It's true that the basic calories in-calories out relationship is the foundation of dieting, but aspartame messes with that. Research is ongoing in this area, but it appears that aspartame affects brain and body chemistry to the point where it can cause more weight gain than even ingesting sugar. If you must use an artificial sweetener, try one like stevia that isn't really artificial at all—it's an extract from a plant that has no calories. It's actually more of a sugar substitute than an artificial sweetener.

Keep a food journal. By recording everything you eat, you may be able to recognize a pattern that is related to your weight loss plateau. You may realize that every time you eat a

The Atkins Diet - 51

certain food, even if it is on the Atkins list of acceptable foods, you gain a little bit of weight or can't seem to lose anymore. You may also notice things like holidays, events, or hormonal cycles that can account for your loss of steam.

Try going back a step or two. The great thing about the Atkins diet is that you can tailor it to your personal needs. And if you need to go backwards for a little while, that's just fine. Perhaps you were in a hurry to add some foods back to your diet or were a little overly optimistic about keeping to your workout schedule as you ramped up your carbs again. Consider going back to before you added a few foods or even back to the induction phase. If you start losing weight again, you'll know it's something you re-eliminated from your diet that was causing you to plateau.

Try some new foods. Everyone's body responds differently to food. Maybe it's time to swap out some of your go-to foods for something new to see if that can boost your metabolism or maybe just give you more energy during your workouts to burn a few extra calories. The Atkins diet list of acceptable foods is pretty extensive, especially in the later phases of the diet, so there are bound to be foods you haven't tried yet. Another suggestion is to try preparing dietary staples in new ways. Some ideas for vegetables, for example, include:

- sprinkle fresh herbs on your salad or change your base greens

- try sautéing instead of steaming or vice versa

- roast your vegetables in the oven or throw them on the grill

- repurpose vegetables: instead of using avocados in dips or salads, try them as a base for dessert dishes

- eat vegetables that you'd normally cook raw instead

Change your workout. Sometimes doing the same old workout can cause you to get a bit lazy about it or not put quite the same oomph into it as before. If that's the case, try upping the intensity for a while. Also, when your body adapts to a certain exercise regimen, it can stop burning the calories it did when you initially started. A good solution for this problem is to change up your routine. Instead of running every day, alternate your jog with a yoga class. Replace three days of weight machines with tennis, swimming, or bicycling. When you keep your body guessing about what comes next, you get a metabolic boost.

Time your eating and exercise periods properly. Speaking of metabolic boosts, did you know that you get one for an hour or two after you exercise? Instead of eating before you workout, consider having a small snack before exercise and saving your meal for afterward. Likewise, make sure you aren't eating big, heavy meals too close to bedtime. Give yourself time to metabolize some of your food before you hit the sack.

Accept your temporary plateau. If you've tried some of the solutions above, and your weight hasn't budged, don't be too hard on yourself. Perhaps it's time to accept your plateau as a temporary setback that happens to virtually all dieters. Don't use it as an excuse to quit on your diet but rather a chance to catch your breath and congratulate yourself on the weight you've lost so far. Be confident that your plateau will resolve, enjoy a treat from the acceptable foods list, and be proud of yourself for the work you've done to create a new healthy lifestyle for yourself!

CONCLUSION

Thank you again for downloading this book!

I hope this book was able to help you to learn more about the Atkins diet.

The next step is to set a date to start your new eating plan!

Finally, if you enjoyed this book, then I'd like to ask you for a favor, would you be kind enough to leave a review for this book on Amazon? It'd be greatly appreciated!

Thank you and good luck!

Printed in the USA
CPSIA information can be obtained
at www.ICGtesting.com
LVHW021813081223
765938LV00002B/103